HAWAI'I

Mutual
Publishing

To celebrate the Year 2000, Mutual Publishing has designated several of its Fall 1999 and Spring 2000 titles as Millennium books. Each of these titles cover an important aspect of Hawai'i—its culture, history, or beauty, and their subject matter helps commemorate the change of centuries.

Doug Peebles' *Hawai'i* is a collection of his large format and panorama images. As Hawai'i enters the millennium, the protection of its beauty and its pristine places is as important as ever. Peebles' photographic mastery of these locales reminds us of the fragility of our Island home.

HAWAI'I

NORTH
KOHALA
COAST

WAIMEA
CANYON

HAWAI'I

Photography by **Douglas Peebles**

Text by **Jan TenBruggencate**

**Mutual
Publishing**

Library of Congress
Catalog Card Number 99-66389

Book Design
Michael Horton Design

ISBN 1-56647-279-2

First Printing, October 1999
1 2 3 4 5 6 7 8 9

Mutual Publishing
1215 Center Street, Suite 210
Honolulu, Hawaii 96812
Telephone (808) 732-1709
Fax (808) 734-4094
e-mail: mutual@lava.net
www.mutualpublishing.com

Printed in Korea

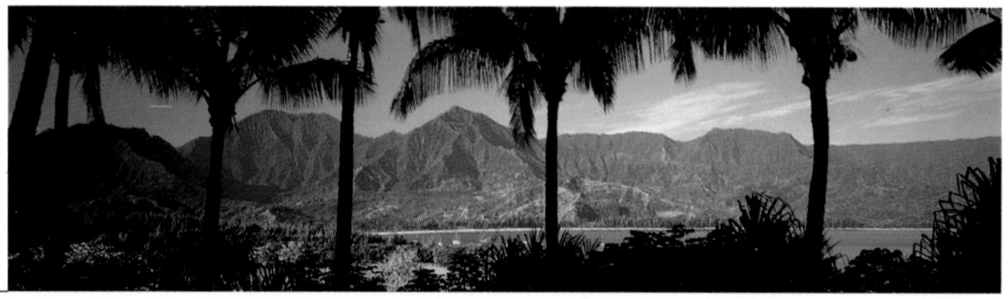

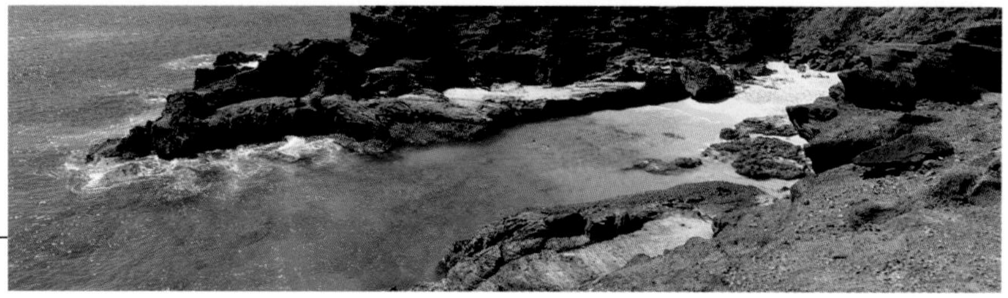

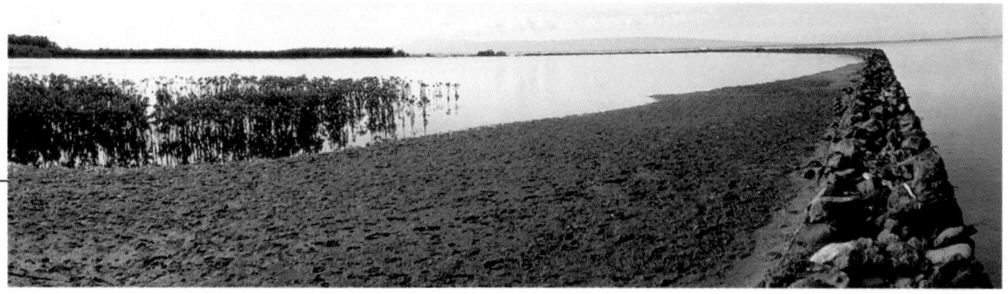

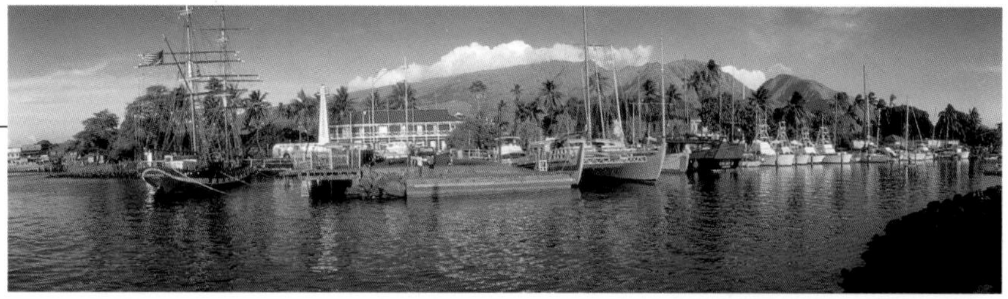

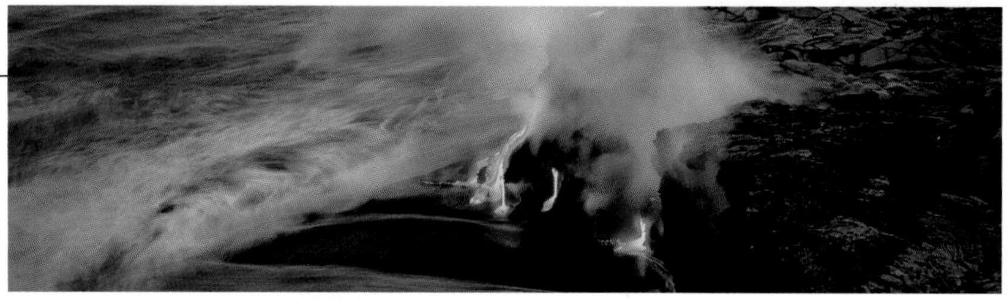

MY
FRONT
YARD

I CAME TO HAWAI'I

from Florida in 1974. I had expected to stay about six months then move to California. Six months later I did not want to leave. I still don't. Living here isn't always paradise but whenever my wife, Margaret, and I talk about going somewhere else, we can't come up with anything.

One of the hard things about Hawaii is finding a good job. I never did. I have been doing freelance photography since I got here. There is a definition of a freelance photographer, as someone with two cameras and a working spouse. I certainly fit that for awhile.

Since then I have done over thirty books on Hawaii covering each of the islands, aerials, flowers, and trees. This book is a little different. I got to choose the photos, with the help of Michael Horton on the final selection. It is somewhat of a "best of" however most of the photos have not been published in a book before. Many of these are from places that I have visited often. The palm tree on this page really is shot from my front yard. I probably have a hundred photos of it. This one is my favorite. In fact that is really what this book is, a selection on my favorite images of Hawaii and its people. I hope you enjoy it.

Technically, these photos were done on three formats. For the panoramics I used a Fuji 6x17. The rest of the photos were done with 35mm Nikons & Canons and a Pentax 6x7.

Douglas Peebles

FOREWORD

HAWAI'I STARTS SMALL,

From an aircraft, it is a spot of gray-green on a blue sea, clouds all around. From the sea, a mountaintop rises, indistinct at first, and then increasingly clear, increasingly real. Those born here see it at first as a small place, a house, a yard, a neighborhood.

But the island expands as far and wide as the viewer is willing to look.

There is enough diversity in Hawai'i that there's always something undiscovered. If the valley is small, you can hike or drive to the next valley. No one has stood under every waterfall, nor enjoyed vistas from every possible vantage. If the island feels small, you can travel to the next island. If all the islands seem small, there is always the endless sea to explore.

An explorer can also look inward for diversity. Narrowing the horizons, oddly, also reveals an expanded world. The smaller are the things you study, the more of them there seem to be.

Some visitors, after a week, assert that they have done Hawai'i, that they have seen it. But many of us after a lifetime of dedication are still seeing it anew. Always in Hawai'i, there is more to see, more to learn, more mystery, more opportunity for study.

KĀNE'OHE
BAY

One of the fascinating subjects is how this place came to be—how it evolved from a pile of smoking lava to a subtropical wonderland that challenges the camera as it challenges the eye. Hawai'i starts small, but it can quickly expand to fill your personal universe. You feel a part of it. People who are recently arrived are notorious for feeling a surge of commitment to the islands, for standing up, willing to fight to protect lifestyle and environment.

KOHALA
COAST
Hawai'i

The place is like that. The place has done all this before.

Each new visitor discovers Hawai'i, unaware that it has been discovered and rediscovered repeatedly across the millennia. And each new visitor changes it.

A newcomer stands on the shore, surrounded by the plants and animals, birds and bugs, fungi and bacteria, and offshore the corals and fishes—the offspring of previous voyagers, previous discoverers. The first-timer stands in the forest, in the shade of the sons and daughters of long-ago travelers.

Hawai'i is thousands of miles from anywhere. It was no easy discovery for any of them. And yet they arrived, one after another. Enough of them to create a complex, interwoven ecosystem thriving on the volcanic rocks.

Which was the first to land on the still-warm lava?

MOLOKA'I
CHANEL

Among the first inhabitants of new lava flows today are small ferns, whose spores dust the surface until some find a place with enough shade, enough moisture, enough of a foothold that the plant will survive. Spores travel constantly in the atmosphere, and could easily have been among the first to arrive. Algae, fungi and mosses, which also reproduce through the production of spores, are other likely candidates.

Or perhaps the winds carried a tiny spider, clinging to a few feet of silk, ripped by a gust from some other land and carried aloft until a downdraft or a sudden rainstorm robbed it of its aerial freedom and returned it to earth.

4

The first arrival might as easily have been a marine creature of some description. The larvae of a wide variety of marine life travel the oceans, part of the complex planktonic clouds that flow with the winds and the currents. Perhaps the original inhabitant was a fish, or an infant coral, or a larval crab.

The skies over the islands are regularly punctuated by migrating and feeding birds. An albatross will fly thousands of miles to find food for its young. Today, some fly from nesting areas in Hawai'i to California bays to feed, and return to their nests repeatedly during the season. Plovers migrate similar distances in search of fast land for winter stays. Even today, migrating ducks somehow find their ways from Mainland areas to Hawai'i. Any of them, stopping while passing by, could have carried a bit of life, like a seed stuck to its feather or in its gut, that could have tried to establish itself in the Islands.

On the sea's surface, a range of land-based life forms clings to survival on floating objects, such as logs, snags, pumice and rafts of vegetation washed out of rivers in stormwaters. Any of these could have made landfall on an Hawaiian shore and crawled or hopped or sent roots into the rocky terrain at the high—water mark. Seeds of some plant species also float, and some of them retain their viability for months.

The possibilities are enormous, and ultimately, it is likely all of these means of introduction succeeded once or many times.

But once arrived, could the life form have gone on to populate these islands? Once here, it faced new a new challenge: surviving alone. Some species certainly could not have, not if only one of them arrived. Plants that require both a male plant and a female plant to reproduce would have had to have waited for a mate. If a plant required a specific kind of bird or insect to pollinate it, it might not have survived even if both male and female flowers were present.

A lost bird might have starved, or lived out a lonely life and died. A fish grown from larval form might have starved on coastal rocks devoid of other life.

Some plants might have been able to survive in a Hawai'i with virtually no other forms of life around. Ferns could have. Lichen. Seaweed. Coral. Whichever was first, the evidence is that the islands were colonized, and colonized repeatedly. Little by little life took hold. One by one, species arrived. It may have taken tens or hundreds of thousands of years between successful introductions, but Hawai'i had the time. The Hawaiian Hot Spot has been pushing islands through the floor of the Pacific Ocean for at least 70 million years—that's the age of the oldest member of the Hawaiian-Emperor chain, Meiji Seamount. As the islands slowly drifted north and west on the moving Pacific Plate, new islands were created behind them.

HOKULEA
SAILING
CANOE

But even with so much time, Hawai'i's isolation kept arrivals from being a common event or an easy one. Scientists note that many entire groups of life forms never made it to the islands. No amphibians, for example. There were virtually no mammals—just the Hawaiian hoary bat and the Hawaiian monk seal. Many species of plant—ones with short-lived seeds, or heavy ones that couldn't float or be carried by a bird—never made the passage.

It would have been difficult for any species to make the 2,500-mile trip from the nearest continent to Hawai'i, but once a bird or plant—or even a bat or seal—was established on one island, the hop to the next island was just a matter of 20 to 60 miles. A mere day's jaunt with a favorable wind or current.

So, while parts of the Big Island are brand new, Maui is a million or so and even Kaua'i is just 5 million years of age, the first arrivals in these islands may have arrived tens of millions of years ago.

They haven't wasted that time. Before the first humans got here, they made good use of their isolation, evolving into unique forms to suit the varied unique microclimates and ecosystems they found. A single finch—perhaps a female carrying a male egg, or perhaps a pair or a small flock—evolved into an array of Hawaiian honeycreepers known to scientists around the world. To suit the

MO'OKINI HEIAU

niches they found in the islands, their colors changed, their bill shapes changed, even their diets changed. Some took to eating fruits, some insects, and some nectar. A few weren't picky, and could make a meal on any of several things.

Hawai'i developed a range of flightless birds, including geese and rails, since the lack of mammalian predators meant it was safe to be on the ground. In fact, flight in some cases might have been a disadvantage, since raptors like the Hawaiian hawk were among the top predators, and since they lacked mice and other small prey, they specialized in taking birds, in flight or from nests in trees.

Plants likewise evolved. Some species, like the Haleakalā silversword, that grew high in the mountains, evolved a coating of silvery hairs that reflected the powerful rays of the sun at higher elevations. There were no grazing mammals, so thorned species stopped wasting energy making thorns. Plants like the beggar's tick, whose seeds had spines to help hitch a ride on passing animals, lost the spines in Hawai'i.

Some plants changed so dramatically that they became nearly unrecognizable as the offspring of their forebears. Some shrubs evolved, for instance, into trees.

By the time the first Polynesian canoe pulled up on an Hawaiian beach between 1,500 and 2,000 years ago, this was a place like no other. And while it has changed dramatically in the intervening years, it remains unique.

Polynesian travelers introduced more than two dozen species of plants, all of them useful. Some were edible, some medicinal, and many had multiple known uses. The canoe voyagers also brought dogs, pigs, chickens and, intentionally or not, rats. Between the people, the new plants and the introduced animals, the change of Hawai'i's landscape speeded up dramatically. Extinction of existing species also speeded up.

TI PLANT

Today, many Hawaiian landscapes contain no native plants at all. A green hillside might sport big old mango trees, vast spreading albizzias, some clumps of fat bamboo, Java plum, silver oak and eucalyptus. None is a native, but all are now permanent parts of the modern Hawaiian environment.

The densest collections of native plants, native birds and native insects are now found generally at high elevations, in the cloud forests around the islands' volcanic peaks. Even here, alien invaders are gaining in numbers. They are the feral pigs—crosses between the Polynesian pigs and thick-chested European varieties released by voyagers on early sailing ships.

There are also ornamental plants gone wild, like the wide-leafed miconia and the blackberry. And alien insects, like more than 40 species of ants, and the mosquitoes that carry avian malaria to Hawai'i's forest birds, few of which tolerate the disease.

The pre-human Hawaiian environment faced infrequent arrivals of new species, and had time to adjust. Today, there's so little time. Wave after wave of new introductions challenge the environmental status quo. The Hawaiian environment is being altered at breakneck pace. What you see today isn't what was here a century ago. What was here then wasn't what was here a millennium ago. And what was here then wasn't here before human contact.

The images in this volume are Hawai'i caught at this moment in time. It wasn't exactly this way before, and won't be thus much longer. Enjoy it.

KAUA'I

Kaua'i, the oldest and northernmost of the main populated Hawaiian islands, is very different from the rest. It has more big running rivers than any of the other islands, all fed from the extraordinarily wet central part of the island. Wai'ale'ale, the name of a mile-high pool at the top of an ancient crater, has laid claim to being the wettest spot on the planet. In some years, it probably is. A federal agency used to keep a giant copper kettle the size of a 55-gallon drum in the sodden sedges near the pool, as a rain gauge. In its best years, Wai'ale'ale has been so wet that the huge rain gauge overflowed, so no accurate record exists of those drenching years. Today, electronic sensors check the rain, which average in excess of 400 inches annually.

All that rain translates into some stunning scenery. Two of the most notable examples are the Waimea Canyon and Nā Pali Coast. The canyon, the result of earth movement and erosion is a 2,000-foot-deep chasm, which lays bare the island's geologic history—layer upon layer of lava, some still hard and black, and many aged to chalky reds and oranges, yellows and purples. Nā Pali, the roadless cliff-and-valley coastline of the northwest-facing side of the island, is clad in dense greens. The hanging valleys and coastal beaches stand amid soaring rock faces

NĀPALI
COAST

and randomly crenelated peaks. A tortuous trail from the north side of the island clings to the faces and sweeps through narrow valleys to reach Kalalau, the largest valley and central gem of Nā Pali. It is a valley that many viewers describe as

HĀʻENA
BEACH

a natural cathedral, not just for its shape but with all the religious connotations of the term.

NĀPALI
COAST

But there is more to Kaua'i. Its beach that starts at Polihale is the longest in the state, a sandy strip that runs fifteen miles around the southwest end of the island, culminating at the Waimea River. This end of the island provides the closest views most visitors will see of the private island of Ni'ihau, where the roughly 200 Hawaiian residents work, play, attend church and educate their kids in the Hawaiian language.

Kaua'i's small towns are mostly the remnants of the sugar and pineapple plantation era, though pineapple is gone and sugar acreage is a fraction of its former size.

WAILUA
FALLS

GIANT
TARO

KALALAU
BEACH

KALALAU
VALLEY

Kaua'i

15

LUMAHAʻI
BEACH

Kauaʻi

MANAWAIPUNA
FALLS

NĀPALI
COAST

Kaua'i

PRINCEVILLE
HANALEI
Following pages

HANALEI
TARO
Previous pages

HANALEI
SUNSET
Kaua'i

25

HANALEI
BAY

WEST KAUA‘I
BEACH

HANALEI
PIER
Kaua'i

KĒ'Ē
Following pages

PO‘IPŪ
SUNSET
Kaua‘i

NĀPALI
COAST
Kaua'i

O'AHU

THE GATHERING PLACE

They call O'ahu the gathering place. Eighty percent of the state's population lives there and Honolulu serves as both the capitol and the state's only major city. On top of that, it has Waikīkī, one of the best-known beaches in the world, backed by a phalanx of tall hotels. For all its urban development, O'ahu is a beautiful island with natural wonders that rank with the best the islands have to offer.

Kāne'ohe Bay, full of islands and picnic sandbars, is a wondrous, reef-protected expanse. To the south, Kailua and Waimanālo bays both sport long white sand beaches and calm, clear waters for all kinds of ocean activities.

Perhaps the best skin-diving habitat in all Hawai'i is at the marine reserve at Hanauma Bay, where fish have been protected from fishing pressure for many years and have grown accustomed to visitors in colorful swim attire.

Visitors watch bodysurfers bash themselves into the bottom at Sandy Beach and surfers wipe out on the other extreme of the island at Sunset Beach. Surfers, divers, jet-skiers, sail-boarders, monohull and multihull sailors, canoe paddlers and canoe sailors and canoe surfers, kayakers and the list goes on. If it's done on the water, they're doing it off O'ahu.

KA'AHUMANU
SOCIETY

The island's less well-known areas include hiking trails through the mountain ranges that form the island's twin spines—the Ko'olau and the Wai'anae mountains. Between them hangs central O'ahu, a broad plain of pineapple fields and other crops, housing projects and the Army's Schofield Barracks. At the south end of the central plain is the remarkable system of harbors that made O'ahu the most

DIAMOND
HEAD *O'ahu*

populous island. Pearl Harbor is the site of the Navy's major Pacific installation, a collection of inland bays and backwaters and the site of the much-visited Arizona Memorial and the retired Battleship Missouri.

Off to the east, next to Honolulu International Airport, is Keʻehi Lagoon, whose dredged seaplane runways are visible from the air, and which is a popular site for sailing, jetski operations and outrigger canoe races. Still farther east is Honolulu

KĀNEʻOHE
BAY

Harbor, where the Hawaiʻi Maritime Museum tells the marine history of the islands. If it's not out voyaging, the Polynesian voyaging canoe Hokuleʻa is moored at the museum. This twin-hulled, 60-footer was the leader in the renaissance of Polynesian canoe voyaging, and after its sailing trips through the Pacific, many South Pacific islanders have built their own big canoes to revive the oceanic traditions of the Islands.

BYODA IN TEMPLE
KAHALUU

'IOLANI
PALACE *O'ahu*

37

MAKAPU'U
Previous pages

HĀLONA
BEACH

ARIZONA
MEMORIAL
Oahu

OUTRIGGER
SAILING
CANOE

LANIKAI
Following pages

WAIMEA
BAY
O'ahu

HONOLULU
Previous pages

48

NORTH
SHORE
O'ahu

KĀNEʻOHE
BAY

Oʻahu

KĀNE'OHE
BAY *O'ahu*

KĀNE'OHE
BAY *O'ahu*

OLOMANA *Oʻahu*

HAU'ULA

HANAUMA
BAY

KAHANA

Oʻahu

WAIKĪKĪ *Oʻahu*

PALI
LOOKOUT
O'ahu

WAIKĪKĪ
O'ahu

LĀNAʻI
MOLOKAʻI

THE PINEAPPLE ISLAND

Pineapple made modern Lānaʻi, but while there's still a field of pineapple out in front of the airport, tourism is its economic engine today. Drive by the luxurious hotel called The Lodge at Kōʻele, in the shade of Lānaʻi's trademark Norfolk Island pines, and you're reminded of an old English manor. The Mānele Bay Hotel at Hulopoʻe Bay is a classy Hawaiian beach resort. But once you leave the confines of either one, you find yourself in old Lānaʻi, a place of dust and history.

KAUNALŪ
LĀNAʻI

Most of the roads on the island are dirt paths that lead to fascinating places. Head northwest from Lānaʻi City to reach the Garden of the Gods, a testament to erosion, where ancient volcanic stones stand stark on a red clay landscape. The route north on the Keōmuku Road leads from paved to dirt and sand, and bounces along the windward coastline of the island, past weekend houses and fishing camps, and the abandoned village of Keōmuku. In the winter and spring, from these shores you can watch the whales playing between Maui, Molokaʻi, Kahoʻolawe and Lānaʻi.

HUELO ISLAND
MOLOKAʻI

Hulopoʻe Bay to the south is a marine life sanctuary and one of the prettiest protected beaches in the state. Swimmers here are likely to be joined by dolphins. Nearby is the site of the historic village of Kaunolū, where the conqueror Kamehameha spent summers. One of the most fascinating features here is Kahekili's Jump, a place where Hawaiian daredevils would leap into the ocean from a 60-foot cliff. To survive, they needed to have enough forward momentum to clear a 15-foot ledge at the bottom of the cliff.

The heart of the island is the mountains above Lāna'i City, where a small crown of native rainforest leads to the 3,370-foot elevation of the summit, Lāna'ihale. The Munro Trail through the high country is named after George C. Munro, the former ranch manager who planted the Norfolks.

The 9-mile channel called Kalohi separates Lāna'i from ancient Moloka'i, another former

pineapple island, famous in Hawaiian tradition for its powerful priests. Here are wide beaches, friendly people and the clifftop vista over Kalaupapa, the 19th century Hansen's disease settlement.

West Moloka'i celebrates the island's cattle ranching and pineapple traditions. The old town of Maunaloa has museums and the remains of the old Libby's pineapple plantation, along with one of the state's top arenas for rodeos. Visitors will find opportunities for backcountry bike riding and horseback activities, as well as a range of shoreline sports.

WAIKOLO
MOLOKA'I

HAWAIIAN
FISHPOND

Moloka'i

KALAUPAPA

WAIKOLU
PRESERVE
TRAIL

Molokai

KAPUAĪWA
COCONUT
GROVE

Moloka'i

NORTH
COASTLINE

Moloka'i

MOA'ULA
FALLS

Moloka'i

CANOE
RACE

Moloka'i

PĀPŌHAKU

Moloka'i

PETROGLYPH *Lāna'i*

POLIHUA
BEACH
COASTLINE

Lāna'i

SUNSET

Lāna'i

MAUI

THE VALLEY ISLE

The million-year-old volcano of Haleakalā rises to more than 10,000 feet over east Maui, and although it may look dead, it's not. It last erupted in the late 1700s, and geologists estimate it could go off again at any time. But don't hold your breath; estimates in geological time are notorious for keeping folks waiting.

Haleakalā's summit provides visitors and residents alike with one spectacle outside its own grandeur—the rising of the sun, viewed from high above most of the salt spray and dust of lower elevations. The mountain's name translates "house of the sun," and in legend, here is where the demigod Maui kidnapped the sun to coerce it to spend a little more time in the sky each day.

Come down off the mountain and turn right, and a twisting ribbon of road carries a visitor from vista to vista on the road to the tiny community of Hāna at the eastern end of the island.

Maui has another mountain, separated from Haleakalā by a fertile isthmus. The heart of the island's visitor industry lies along the southern shore, in the lee created by both Haleakalā and the West Maui Mountains. These calm waters are not only

SUNSET AT
KĪHEI

favorites of tourists, but of Hawai'i's renowned winter residents, the humpback whales, which leave their summer feeding grounds off Alaska for calving and cavorting around Hawai'i.

Whale watching is one of Maui's biggest visitor activities, with research vessels and sailing cruises heading out among them throughout the season. The town of Lahaina, once a center of the whaling industry of the 1800s, still celebrates whales

ʻĪAO NEEDLE

PROTEA *Maui*

but now in a way that's less destructive to the big mammals. After Honolulu, the south Maui coastline is the state's most active visitor area, full of historic and recreational attractions. Tourists can shop, kayak, sail or even hang from a parachute behind a speedboat.

Divers can take boats out to the little crescent of Molokini, an old volcanic tuff cone whose crater features fine coral reef habitat and has fish populations protected as a marine reserve. Beyond Molokini is the dry island of Kahoʻolawe, a former military bombing range now being restored as an Hawaiian cultural icon. Kahoʻolawe lies in the lee of Haleakalā, and is deprived of the rainfall that greens up many of the other islands.

WATERFALL *Maui*

LAHAINA

HALEAKALĀ
CRATERS

ROAD TO
HALEAKALĀ *Maui*

HALEAKALĀ
SUNRISE

KĪPAHULU
Following pages

ROAD TO
HĀNA

HĀNA
COAST

MĀKENA
BEACH
Previous pages

WAI'ĀNAPANAPA *Maui*

KEALAIKAHIKI
POINT *Kaho'olawe*

HOʻOKIPA
BEACH
Previous pages

KĀ'ANAPALI

Maui

MOLOKINI
ISLAND

HĀNA
COAST

THE BIG ISLAND

HAWAI'I

The newest of the Hawaiian islands is a massive volcanic structure, with five old connected volcanoes: Mauna Kea, Mauna Loa, Kīlauea, Hualālai and Kohala, plus the old volcano of Mahukona, whose summit lies underwater off the northwest side of the island and whose flanks are buried under the lavas of the Kohalas and Hualālai.

The island is so diverse that it is difficult to describe in short. Live volcanoes at Kīlauea, Mauna Loa and Hualālai, dense rainforests on windward slopes, a vast volcanic desert at Ka'ū. Cowboy traditions on the pastured Waimea uplands, coffee and macadamia nut orchards overlooking the leeward coastlines of Kona. Prizewinning gamefishing off the Kailua coast, world-class astronomy on the often snowy summit of Mauna Kea. An active flower-growing industry, as well as an active, illicit marijuana-growing trade. Upscale resorts at South Kohala and a thriving counterculture in Puna.

PARKER
RANCH

Island residents sometimes argue about whether to split the governance of Hawai'i in two, with capitols at the very different centers of Hilo and Kailua-Kona.

Hilo is an old town on the wet windward side, home to the island's major harbor at the base of the Hāmākua Coast, which was once a vast sugar-growing region. The configuration of the bottom of Hilo Bay has twice focused destructive tsunami onto the shore here, and the Tsunami Museum now recalls those tragedies. The Hilo region includes the diversified agricultural fields of Hāmākua and Puna, the Hawai'i Volcanoes National Park and its environs, Mauna Kea and the Waipi'o end of the cliff and valley cluster off the windward side of the Kohala Mountains.

104

NĒNĒ
GOOSE

Kona is the sunnier side, where calm waters favor fishing and easy shoreline recreation. The luxury hotels of the South Kohala region form oases in the dry lava fields. Coffee, macadamia nuts and pastures run up the sides of Mauna Loa and Hualālai, a region supplied with numerous historic villages with aging wood-frame structures. The high region between the Kohala Mountains and Mauna Kea is the heart acreage of the vast Parker Ranch, whose headquarters at Waimea (some call it Kamuela) have turned it into an eclectic town of cowboys and astronomers and retirees.

PU'UHONUA
O HŌNAUNAU

ALAHAKA
BAY
Hawai'i

KOHALA
SUNSET
Previous pages

'AMA'U
TREE
FERN

Hawai'i

'AKAKA
FALLS

Hawai'i

LAPAKAHI
STATE PARK

HAWAI'I
VOLCANOES
NATIONAL
PARK
Hawai'i

116

PUNA
COASTLINE
Hawai'i

KĪLAUEA LAVA
FLOWS INTO
THE OCEAN
Previous pages

KĪLAUEA

LAVA

FLOW

Hawai'i

120

KĪLAUEA
ERUPTION
Hawai'i

KĪLAUEA
LAVA
FLOWS

Hawai'i

SNOW CAPPED
MAUNA KEA
Following pages

123

PUʻUHONUA
O HŌNAUNAU

Hawaiʻi

RAINBOW
FALLS

PUNALUʻU
BLACK SAND
BEACH

HAWAI'I—SITE DESCRIPTIONS

NORTH KOHALA COAST, HAWAI'I p. iii

The trade winds and seas beat constantly at this northern coast of the island of Hawai'i, constantly eroding the rock cliffs. Moist winds driven up the cliff faces generate high rainfall, which in turn feeds dozens of waterfalls. No roads cross this rough terrain, but there are foot and mule trails built by early Hawaiians and by sugar planters seeking water for their crops.

WAIMEA CANYON, KAUA'I p. v

Sometimes called the Grand Canyon of the Pacific, this extensive system of deep valleys displays the remarkable effects of erosion. Layers of lavas of different chemical makeups have aged and weathered into soils and rocks in a range of earth tones. The canyon floor in many areas is covered with Hawaiian stone agricultural terraces. Waimea means "red water," and refers to soil sediment in the water.

KOHALA COAST, HAWAI'I p. 3

The native Hawaiian connection to the elements is strong. The earth, sky, sea, plants, animals and humans were all seen as an interrelated continuum. Here, a practitioner of the ancient *hula* chants and beckons from the land to the sea.

HĀ'ENA BEACH, KAUA'I p. 11

The rugged cliffs of Hā'ena were made familiar the world wide in the movie "South Pacific." They form the boundary between the parts of Kaua'i that are accessible by vehicle and those parts that must be navigated on foot or reached from the sea. Hā'ena means "red hot."

WAILUA FALLS, KAUA'I p. 12

The Wailua River drains much of eastern Kaua'i, including the waters plunging over the cliffs from Wai'ale'ale, the reputed wettest spot on Earth. At this scenic point, the falls pour over a 200-foot cliff into a broad plunge pool. There are two major tributaries feeding the main river course, which may explain Wailua's meaning, "two waters."

KALALAU BEACH, KAUA'I p. 13

The largest valley on Kaua'i's Nā Pali coastline is Kalalau, whose floor is a maze of old *taro* terraces. It is now a popular state park, which campers reach by taking an 11-mile cliffside trail from Hā'ena.

Kalalau's stream reaches the sea over a bed of rounded boulders, but there is a sand beach as well. The name means "the straying."

GIANT TARO, KAUA'I p. 13

Hawai'i's forests are filled with a combination of native plants and ones introduced by humans. This relative of the *taro*—'*ape* or elephant ear—grows in wet forest understories and was brought to the islands. While not preferred, its root could be eaten after long cooking. Its leaves are huge, and can be used as a makeshift umbrella in an unexpected rainfall.

KALALAU VALLEY, KAUA'I pp. 14-15

Kalalau, viewed from its 4,000-foot elevation back rim, is a vast amphitheater valley. Near-vertical cliffs cut by waterfalls drop to a wide valley floor. An ancient trail once led down to the valley from the mountains at Kōke'e, but erosion and dense cliffside vegetation have obliterated it. The valley is now reached from a coastal trail or by sea.

LUMAHA'I BEACH, KAUA'I pp. 16-17

The sandy, north-facing Lumaha'i features a beach broken by rocky outcroppings. In winter, storms in the North Pacific drive huge swells onto this coastline, but it is a favorite of visitors when the sea is calm. The nearest crescent in this view was Nurse's Beach in the movie "South Pacific."

MANAWAIPUNA FALLS, KAUA'I p. 18

Deep in Hanapēpē Valley, this beautiful cascade was little known until the makers of the film "Jurassic Park" used it as a backdrop. Today, it is on the standard tour of Kaua'i's several helicopter firms. It drops into a plunge pool and then runs over a rocky stream bottom to join the Hanapēpē River. The name refers to a stream branch spring.

NĀ PALI COAST, KAUA'I p. 19

Early Hawaiians lived along the rugged coastline of northwestern Kaua'i, growing *taro* and other crops on the stream-fed valley floors, fishing along the shore when ocean conditions allowed it. When possible, they traveled by outrigger canoe. But an alternative was foot trails that ran along the cliffs. In one location, a coconut trunk served as a ladder between trail sections. Nā Pali means "the cliffs."

PRINCEVILLE HANALEI, KAUA'I pp. 20-21

A protective reef keeps the shoreline water calm much of the time at the base of the Princeville cliffs. Here, isolated patches of sand provide access to good snorkeling and swimming, and some beach-goers ride body boards in the surf. The region was named for the royal son of Kamehameha IV, who died young.

HANALEI TARO, KAUA'I pp. 22-23

The broad flatlands of lower Hanalei Valley are extensively irrigated for the cultivation of *taro*, a plant favored across the Pacific, but which reached its peak of cultivation in Hawai'i, where dozens of varieties were established. Every part of the *taro* plant is eaten, but it is the thick corm that is beaten into *taro's* best-known product, *poi*. The name Hanalei refers to the curved bay at the mouth of the valley.

HANALEI SUNSET, KAUA'I pp. 24-25

The view across Hanalei Bay at the end of the day is one of the most romantic in all Hawai'i. In the foreground, the famous *hala* trees, whose leaves were woven into mats and sails for canoes by the early residents of these islands. *Hala,* also known as pandanus or screwpine, was once among the most common coastal trees of the region.

HANALEI BAY, KAUA'I pp. 26-27

The north-facing bay of Hanalei is a dangerous place for boats during the high surf of winter, but from the end of May to the beginning of September, it is a favored anchorage for local boats and for yachts from around the world. The Singlehanded Transpac yacht race, held every other year, finishes here.

WEST KAUA'I BEACH, KAUA'I pp. 28-29

The coast of Kaua'i is dotted with private spots. They are patches of sand and pebble, enclosed by protective reefs of coral and basalt. Special spots shaded by palms and heliotrope, *kiawe* and ironwood. Places sought out by beachcombers or sun-seekers, shell-collectors or those looking for a quiet place to read a book.

HANALEI PIER, KAUA'I p. 29

The old pier jutting into the eastern side of Hanalei Bay from Black Pot Park was once used for the loading of crops grown in Hanalei Valley, such as rice and sugar. Today it is no longer used for commercial purposes, but has been restored as a place where local kids jump into the blue water and where visitors and old folks stop to meditate.

KĒʻĒ, KAUAʻI pp. 30-31

At the very end of the road past Hanalei on the north shore of Kauaʻi is Kēʻē, an area and beach whose name means the "avoidance," perhaps because it was so remote in the days before roads. It had a safe canoe landing at the northern end of the cliffs of Nā Pali, a small sand-bottom lagoon protected by reefs. Today Kēʻē is a popular recreational beach, and the starting point for the Kalalau trail.

POʻIPŪ SUNSET, KAUAʻI p. 32

The leeward side of Kauaʻi is most often sunny and the waters usually calm, which belies its name. Poʻipū refers to overcast skies or crashing surf. This is one of the tourism centers of the island, but along the coast, visitors can always find a moment of solitude, particularly at sunset.

NĀ PALI COAST, KAUAʻI p. 33

Artists often take up the challenge of reproducing the stark grandeur of Nā Pali, where seas crash against the base of cliffs and ridgelines march down to the sea. This view, from Kēʻē, looks across the calm lagoon, past a narrow natural channel in the reef toward the large valleys of Hanakāpiʻai, Hanakoa and Kalalau.

DIAMOND HEAD, OʻAHU p. 35

Waikīkī Beach begins just at the base of Diamond Head, which reportedly got its English name from natural crystals found there. They were not diamonds. Its Hawaiian name, Lēʻahi, is believed to be a shortened form of the name Laeʻahi, which compares the crater's shape the brow of a variety of tuna known as ʻahi.

ʻIOLANI PALACE, OʻAHU p. 37

The only royal palace in the United States, ornate ʻIolani Palace was built in the late 1800s, and incorporated stones from a previous royal building on the site as well as stones from a temple at Puna, Hawaʻi. Hawaiian kings and queens lived here, and the last queen, Liliʻuokalani, was imprisoned here after her 1893 overthrow. It has been restored and visitors can experience its royal ambience.

MAKAPUʻU, OʻAHU pp. 38-39

Oʻahu's eastern point, Makapuʻu, features a beach park whose breaks are favorites of surfers. Its name can refer to the start of a hill, or may translate as "bulging eye," recalling the name of an image once kept in a cave near here. Sea Life Park, where visitors can view many kinds of marine life in tanks, pools and aquariums, is located here. The humped offshore island is Rabbit Island or Mānana, and the low rock islet nearer shore is Kāohikaipu.

HĀLONA BEACH, OʻAHU pp. 40-41

Tide pools and stark rock features mark Hālona Beach, next to and below Oʻahu's blowhole, between Hanauma Bay and Sandy Beach. This rugged section of the island is regularly pounded by heavy surf that wraps around the south side of eastern Oʻahu after passing through the notoriously rough Molokaʻi Channel.

ARIZONA MEMORIAL, OʻAHU p. 42

The National Park Service operates the memorial to the sailors killed in Japan's Dec. 7, 1941, attack on Pearl Harbor, which launched the United States into World War II. Ferries take visitors out to the memorial, which is built atop the sunken USS Arizona. The war ended Sept. 2, 1945, when Japanese officials surrendered aboard the the USS Missouri, the retired battleship that is anchored within sight of the Arizona Memorial.

OUTRIGGER SAILING CANOE, OʻAHU p. 43

Early Hawaiians are believed to have sailed to the islands in double-hulled canoes, and frequently navigated between them in their double-hulled vessels or outrigger canoes. Modern-day residents compete in inter-island sailing races aboard vessels much like those used by the early voyagers. The boats are propelled by sails and paddles, and a steersman guides the boat using a paddle.

LANIKAI, OʻAHU pp. 44-45

An offshore reef protects a broad section of Oʻahu's coastline, creating one of the most splendid calm-water recreational areas in the state. This section of the coast, between Kailua and Waimānalo, was originally known as Kaʻōhao, but was renamed Lanikai by a developer who apparently wanted it to mean "heavenly sea," but combined the words so they mean "sea-sky" or "sea-heaven."

HONOLULU, OʻAHU pp. 46-47

Honolulu became the capitol city largely because it has the best-protected harbors in the state both Honolulu Harbor and the complex of lagoons that became Pearl Harbor. The heart of downtown runs inland from the docks of Honolulu Harbor. Aloha Tower, once the city's tallest structure, is now dwarfed by high-rises. Honolulu, appropriately, means "protected bay."

WAIMEA BAY, OʻAHU pp. 48-49

This northern bay fronting a white sand beach has two distinct faces. During much of the summer, it is a clear, calm place for swimming, snorkeling and snoozing. But big winter surf turns Waimea into a raging cauldron known worldwide in the surfing community. Some of the world's biggest surfable waves roll in here. Its name, like Waimea on Kauaʻi, means "red water."

NORTH SHORE, OʻAHU p. 49

Surfers haul out their big boards for the combers that roll during winter into the North Shore of Oʻahu, site of some of the biggest surfing competitions. The hazardous sport has become one of the premier spectator sports as well, and visitors flock to the beaches of the region with binoculars and cameras with long lenses to watch the wild rides and wipeouts.

KĀNEʻOHE BAY, OʻAHU pp. 50-53

Kāneʻohe is one of the largest bays on the island, and despite facing into the prevalent tradewinds, it is generally safe for water activities as the result of a broad barrier reef, the only one of its kind in the islands. It is separated from Kailua Bay by the Mōkapu Peninsula. The area's name means "bamboo husband," and recalls a man whose cruelty was compared to the blade of a bamboo knife. The bay contains several islets, including one, Mokoliʻi, whose shape has been compared to that of a Chinese worker's hat.

OLOMANA, OʻAHU p. 54

Beautiful Olomana is a basalt spire overlooking Kailua. It is a favorite area for hikers. The mountain is named for a legendary giant, who in Hawaiian tradition leaped from Kauaʻi to here. There are other inter-island transits in legend, including a rock, Pōhaku O Kauaʻi, at Kaʻena on Oʻahu, which was believed to have been thrown from Kauaʻi by another giant named Hāʻupu.

HAUʻULA, OʻAHU p. 55

The windward side of Oʻahu has a number of small communities nestled between the steep mountains of the Koʻolau Range and the shore. Hauʻulaʻs waters are favored for catching squid and other forms of reef life. A popular beach park is found here. The areaʻs name means "red *hau*," referring to a relative of the hibiscus which yielded medicine and whose inner bark was used for cordage.

HANAUMA BAY, OʻAHU pp. 56-57

This nicely-protected bay near Koko Head may be the most sought-after piece of coastline in Hawaiʻi, after Waikīkī. It is a protected marine reserve, and fishing is prohibited. Diving and reef walking here is so popular that city and state officials have established strict rules of access to protect the resource. Its name can mean "curved bay," or "hand-wrestling bay."

KAHANA, OʻAHU pp. 58-59

Many of the coconut groves around the state were planted when production of copra, dried coconut meat, was a commercial industry in Hawaiʻi. The copra market has declined, but the trees, among the most useful of plants to Pacific peoples, still stand. The trees are known as *niu* in Hawaiian and produce food, drink, cordage, timber, bait, implements, roofing and more.

WAIKĪKĪ, OʻAHU pp. 60-63

The heart of Hawaiʻi tourism, Waikīkī sports calm waters, the landmark Diamond Head, and the famed Pink Lady, a nickname for the aging but graceful Royal Hawaiian Hotel. In the near-shore waters, surfing, sailing and canoeing add to the ambience. At night, the activity moves from the beach to the streets and showrooms, as the resort community lights up and comes alive with an international blend of entertainment and dining. Waikīkī means "spouting water," and may refer to the many springs in the region before the digging of the Ala Wai, the canal that drained the region.

PALI LOOKOUT, OʻAHU p. 64

The tradewinds blowing into Hawaiʻi from the northeast are driven up the sides of the Koʻolau Mountains, and at the Nuʻuanu Pali Lookout create gusts strong enough to stagger the unwary. Here, travelers once took a tortuous cliffside road from Honolulu to Kailua, but now travel a freeway complete with matched tunnels through the mountain. Pali means "cliff."

WAIKĪKĪ, OʻAHU pp. 64-65

Early Hawaiians excelled at water sports, and developed body surfing, board surfing and canoe surfing. Tourists at Waikīkī take advantage of the skills of modern Hawaiʻi beachboys and catch rides on the gentle waves off the popular beach. Expert canoe paddlers often take on much steeper waves in other parts of the islands.

HAWAIIAN FISHPOND, MOLOKAʻI p. 68

Early Hawaiians learned that they could improve the productivity of their near-shore waters by building huge fishponds, enclosing several acres of water with a boulder and rubble wall, using gated openings to allow fresh water to flow in and out. Here they grew favored fishes and kept out predators. Several old fishponds on Molokaʻi have been restored.

KALAUPAPA, MOLOKAʻI p. 69

The low peninsula called Makanalua juts from the base of Molokaʻiʻs rugged northern cliffs. Here, in the 1800s, the Hawaiian kingdom established a settlement for those suffering from Hansenʻs Disease or leprosy. The disease can now be entirely controlled and there is no need to sequester patients, but a few choose to remain. Fewer than 100 elderly patients still live at Kalaupapa, which means "flat plain."

WAIKOLU PRESERVE TRAIL, MOLOKAʻI pp. 70-71

The Nature Conservancy of Hawaii acquired and protected the rainforests at the summit of Molokaʻi. Here, a complex community of native plants, birds, insects and other forms of life interact. A wooden walkway has been established to allow researchers, students and others access to the area without damaging the delicate environment. Waikolu, the name of the valley and stream that drop from this mountainous area, means "three waters."

KAPUAĪWA COCONUT GROVE, MOLOKAʻI p. 72

The coconut trees of this stand outside Kaunakakai are believed to be more than 130 years old, having been planted in the 1860s for Kamehameha V, who had a home near where the present-day Kaunakakai Pier stands. Kapuaīwa means "mysterious taboo" or "prohibition." The word taboo comes from a word found throughout Polynesia, whose Hawaiian spelling is *kapu*.

NORTH COASTLINE, MOLOKAʻI p. 73

A vast section of the north coast of the island fell away into the sea, leaving a rugged line of cliffs, some of which are nearly half a mile high. Surveys of the ocean floor to the north reveal the rubble of the massive landslide. A waterfall along these cliffs, Kahiwa, drops 1,700 feet. The region was once populated, despite being pounded by rough surf during the winter, which made canoe travel impossible.

MOAʻULA FALLS, MOLOKAʻI p. 74

The east end of Molokaʻi is cut by numerous streams, many of which contain waterfalls such as Moaʻula, one of several that drop into Hālawa Valley. In the plunge pool at the base of the falls, there is a tradition that it is safe to swim if a *ti* leaf thrown on the water floats, and dangerous if it is drawn below the surface. Moaʻula means "red jungle fowl."

CANOE RACE, MOLOKAʻI pp. 74-75

Standard Hawaiian racing canoes seat six paddlers and are supported by two cross members and a float called an *ama*. Canoe hulls, originally made out of various woods, although the hardwood *koa* was preferred for its durability, are now commonly fashioned of fiberglass. The premier race is the Molokaʻi Hoe, in which paddlers take their canoes from west Molokaʻi to Waikīkī Beach on Oʻahu.

PĀPOHAKU, MOLOKAʻI p. 76

A two-mile stretch of white sand faces the island of Oʻahu on the west end of Molokaʻi. The windswept strand was once all but inaccessible, but is now part of the Kaluakoʻi resort development, and sports a public beach park. Beachcombing here is excellent, but the swimming is treacherous due to tricky currents. The name means "stone fence."

PETROGLYPH, LĀNAʻI p. 77

The Hawaiian people had no written language, but left numerous stone carvings whose meanings are still not known. Many are stylized human figures and recognizable animals. Canoes and sails are also found, and in more recent figures, such things as horses and goats. But there were also mysterious symbols, such as circles and dots within circles.

POLIHUA BEACH COASTLINE, LĀNAʻI p. 78

The northernmost beach on the island of Lānaʻi has a sandy beach that serves as a nesting area for sea turtles. Its name, meaning "a bosom for eggs," suggests the early Hawaiians knew this. As with other windward coastlines, Polihua's safety for turtles is threatened by masses of marine debris that wash onto the reef and beach, including nets and ropes that can entangle the animals.

SUNSET, LĀNAʻI p. 79

The island of Lānaʻi was once a part of a massive island called Maui Nui, which included the volcanoes that now form Maui, Molokaʻi, Lānaʻi, Kahoʻolawe and perhaps a sunken volcano off west Molokaʻi now known as Penguin Banks. Sea level rise and the subsidence of the volcanoes drowned the saddles between them, creating independent islands. An alternate name for the island is Nānaʻi.

ʻIAO NEEDLE, MAUI p. 81

The erosion of volcanic landscapes often creates dramatic forms such as deeply incised valleys and towering spires. The ʻIao Needle is such a feature, cut by the waters that flow into the ʻIao Stream. The needle's name means "cloud supreme," considerably different from an alternate name, Kūkaemoku, which translates "cut dung."

PROTEA, MAUI p. 82

The uplands of Maui on the slopes of Haleakalā are a famed agricultural area, where sweet onions and other vegetables compete for space with a flower industry. Among the most impressive of the blooms is the protea, several varieties of which thrive in the Kula region.

LAHAINA, MAUI pp. 84-85

The old whaling town of Lahaina was once the capitol of Hawaiʻi, a rough and tumble town on the protected southern shore of West Maui. The better harbor at Honolulu eventually moved the capitol to Honolulu, but Lahaina has remained a top destination for visitors. Irrigation has greened up the area, but in the days before piped water, its name, meaning "cruel sun," was perhaps more appropriate.

HALEAKALĀ, MAUI pp. 86-89

Maui's eastern volcano, Haleakalā, is a vast rock structure. A seemingly endless winding road leads up its broad side, through sugar fields, then pasture and finally into rocky terrain where unusual species like the compact silverswords reign. The 10,023 foot summit overlooks a broad crater marked with numerous cinder cones and lava fields. The name means "house of the sun," and residents and visitors alike drive up the mountain before dawn to reach the top in time for the view of the sunrise.

KĪPAHULU, MAUI pp. 90-91

Rich volcanic soils and abundant rainfall have turned the Kīpahulu region, between Hāna and Kaupō on the east slopes of Haleakalā, into a tropical jungle. Kīpahulu Valley is part of the Haleakalā National Park, which protects the native ecosystems found in the verdant valley. The pools of ʻOheʻo Gulch, shown here, were once called the Seven Sacred Pools and are a favored swimming area of the region.

HĀNA, MAUI pp. 92-93

Innumerable streams cut the slopes of east Haleakalā, and the twisting road to Hāna crosses more than 50 bridges along its course. The shoreline is one marked by the processes of erosion. Volcanic coastal cliffs and near-shore rocks are pounded by surf, but because of heavy rainfall still sprout with greenery. Hāna can mean "alert."

MĀKENA BEACH, MAUI pp. 94-95

South of the Kīhei resort area are the broad beaches of Mākena. Although this is an arid part of the island, the name of the beach means "abundance," perhaps for the wealth of near-shore marine life. It is a favorite spot for visitors and residents alike to enjoy the sun and calm seas.

WAIʻĀNAPANAPA, MAUI pp. 96-97

This rugged section of the Hāna coastline of Maui has been made a state park, largely for the water-filled caves found here. One of the caves can only be entered by swimming underwater. Tradition holds that the waters of Waiʻānapanapa turn red once each year, in memory of the bloody murder by a chief of his wife, who had swum into the cave to hide from him. The name of the area means "glistening water."

KEALAIKAHIKI POINT, KAHOʻOLAWE p. 97

A canoe leaving Maui or Molokaʻi for the islands of the South Pacific might travel between Kahoʻolawe and Lānaʻi. The name of the channel here is Kealaikahiki, and the name of the westernmost point of Kahoʻolawe has the same name. The name means "the way to Kahiki," which may refer to any of several islands to the south.

HOʻOKIPA BEACH, MAUI pp. 98-99

The strong winds blowing along the shore near the bay called Hoʻokipa, on the Hāna road east of Pāʻia, have made it one of the premier spots for windsurfers from around the world. Before people added sails to surfboards, it was it was best known as a board surfing spot. Its name means "to entertain" or "to be hospitable."

KĀʻANAPALI, MAUI pp. 100-101

The West Maui mountains create a lee to the south and west, protecting the coastline and the near-shore waters from high winds and rough seas that rush through the Pailolo Channel between Maui and Molokaʻi. The area was sometimes called Pōhaku-Kāʻanapali, for a concave-faced stone in the area whose climbing was a special challenge.

MOLOKINI ISLAND p. 101

One of several volcanic tuff cones across the state, Molokini lies between Maui and Kahoʻolawe, and its submerged central crater is a favored diving area for its spectacular corals and fishes. State officials installed permanent moorings after the anchors from the many tour vessels began damaging the reef.

HĀNA COAST, MAUI pp. 102-103

Severe changes in temperature and elevation, in rainfall patterns, in wind regimes and sunlight have created myriad microclimates in the Hawaiian environment. Over time, each has evolved with a unique array of life forms able to best take advantage of the conditions of the location. Here, along the Hāna coastline, plants coexist in an extremely moist, shaded environment.

NĒNĒ GOOSE, HAWAIʻI p. 105

The nēnē is the Hawaiʻi state bird. It evolved from a migrating North American goose to a species unique to the islands. It was once common, but by the middle of the 1900s had become quite rare, in part due to habitat loss and attacks by cats, dogs and mongoose, none of which is native to Hawaiʻi. A captive propagation program helped bring the species back. They are readily seen on Maui, Hawaiʻi and Kauaʻi.

PUʻUHONUA O HŌNAUNAU, HAWAIʻI p. 107

The southern point of Hōnaunau Bay was a place where violators of early Hawaiian laws would be protected from punishment, if they could reach it before being captured. It has been preserved as the City of Refuge National Historical Park. Here, a restored temple and carved temple images stand along the shore. Pu'uhonua, fittingly, is the term for a place of refuge.

ALAHAKA BAY, HAWAI'I pp. 108-109

This bay just south of Hōnaunau is off the beaten track but shares with much of the Kona coast generally sunny and calm weather. There are patches of sand, but much of the coastline is comparatively young black lava. Its name means "plank bridge."

KOHALA SUNSET, HAWAI'I pp. 110-111

The west-facing shores of all the Hawaiian islands provide viewers with stunning sunsets, although they are seldom so especially Hawaiian as when framed by a pair of matched coconut palms. Many viewers make a quest out of looking for the green flash, an emerald flash of sunlight seen on rare clear days the moment the sun disappears over the horizon and when other conditions are perfect.

'AMA'U TREE FERN, HAWAI'I pp. 112-113

One of the most common plants of the Hawaiian forest is the big tree fern known as *hāpu'u*. Another large fern, the *'ama'u*, has fronds simpler in construction than those of the *hāpu'u*. A more delicate-looking tree fern, commonly called the Australia tree fern, is an alien invader in the Hawaiian wet forest, after having been introduced as an ornamental plant.

'AKAKA FALLS, HAWAI'I p. 114

One of the scenic wonders of the islands, 'Akaka Falls is a 440-foot waterfall uphill from the Hāmākua Coast town of Honomū. Visitors walk along a paved pathway amid dense jungle foliage in the 'Akaka Falls State Park to reach the smaller cascade called Kahūnā Falls, and then come upon roaring 'Akaka. The name can mean a "crack" or "separation."

LAPAKAHI STATE PARK, HAWAI'I pp. 114-115

An abandoned fishing village, Koai'e, is now part of the Lapakahi State Historical Park, where visitors learn much about early Hawaiian life and can view archaeological sites, tools and toys, and the plants used by the early inhabitants of the island. A marine preserve here provides a good opportunity to view Hawaiian marine life. Lapakahi means "single ridge."

HAWAI'I VOLCANOES NATIONAL PARK, HAWAI'I p. 116

This park spans Kīlauea and Mauna Loa volcanoes and covers an immense range of landscape, from erupting volcanoes to lava desert where little grows to dense rainforest, shown here. 'Ōhi'a and *koa* trees and tree ferns dominate the wet forest of this region, where native birds still sing. But aggressive alien plants and animals threaten the native forest.

PUNA COASTLINE, HAWAI'I p. 117

The ocean and shoreline vegetation in this section of the Big Island carry on an unending battle. Coastal plants, their roots on rich volcanic soil and fed by plentiful rainfall grow toward the sunlight at the water's edge, only to be driven back by the salt spray that is toxic to them.

KĪLAUEA LAVA FLOWS INTO THE OCEAN, HAWAI'I pp. 118-119

The meeting of molten lava and the rolling sea is accompanied by vast clouds of acid steam. Hot lava shatters into crystals of black sand, explodes into flakes and needles of basalt called Pele's *limu* or seaweed, and Pele's hair, both in honor of the Hawaiian goddess of fire.

KĪLAUEA ERUPTION & LAVA FLOWS, HAWAI'I pp. 120-123

Kīlauea's east rift zone erupted in January 1983 and continued to be the longest continuous eruption of modern times. Millions of cubic meters of rock were deposited on the slopes, and molten rock swept through the communities of Kalapana, Kapa'ahu and Royal Gardens, destroying them. Ancient sites, including the Waha'ula *heiau* complex and the freshwater pond known as Queen's Bath were also covered.

SNOW CAPPED MAUNA KEA, HAWAI'I pp. 124-125

At 13,796 feet, Mauna Kea's summit is the highest spot in the islands. The weather is always cold, but on many winter days, there is enough snow for limited snow skiing. The name of the volcano, appropriately, means "white mountain." And while there are no plants growing up here, a small group of native insects has evolved to fill this ecological niche.

PU'UHONUA O HŌNAUNAU pp. 126-127

Most of Hawai'i's carved statues were destroyed after the Hawaiian kingdom's chiefs converted to Christianity, but a few were secreted away in caves. Others were tossed into swamps whence they were later recovered. Some had been taken by early European voyagers and ended up in museums. Images of some lost carvings were preserved in the drawings of early voyages. The ones shown here are replicas.

HĀMĀKUA COAST, HAWAI'I pp. 128-129

The dense vegetation shown here along the windward coast of the Big Island is almost entirely made up of introduced plants, including the palms. While Hawai'i is renowned for its palms, the only native palm is the *loulu*, a family of fan palms that was once common but now is seldom seen.

RAINBOW FALLS, HAWAI'I p. 130

Waterfalls are among the best places to see rainbows. Perhaps that is why there is a Rainbow Falls in the Great Smoky Mountains of Tennessee, in Washington, in Oregon, in Canada's British Columbia, in New Zealand's Bay of Islands. This waterfall near Hilo is an odd case in which the more common English name accurately translates its Hawaiian name, Wai-anuenue, water of the rainbow.

BLACK SAND BEACH, HAWAI'I p. 131.

Punalu'u Beach on Hawai'i is one of the few accessible black sand beaches left on the Big Island. Famed black sand beaches at Kalapana have been covered over by the lavas of the Pu'u 'O'o eruption on Kīlauea's east rift zone. Most black sand consists of bits of basalt, while white sand beaches are primarily made up of tiny shells, pieces of shell and coral.

Many of the translations of Hawaiian names are from, "Place Names of Hawaii," by Mary Kawena Pukui, Samuel H. Elbert and Esther T. Mookini, University Press of Hawaii, Honolulu.